A
Colour-Rail
Journey

Compiled by Paul Chancellor

Captions by Ron White

PENDRAGON

LMS 2P 4-4-0 No.40563 leads 'West Country' Pacific No.34045 *Ottery St Mary* on a Bradford–Bournemouth train coming off Midford Viaduct. 3rd September 1960. *305792*

First published 2010

ISBN 978 1 899816 18 7

Paul Chancellor, Ron White & Pendragon Publishing 2010

Designed by Barry C. Lane, Sutton-in-Craven

Published by Pendragon Publishing, PO Box 3, Easingwold, York YO61 3YS

Printed by Amadeus Press, Cleckheaton, West Yorkshire

Front Cover

Great North of Scotland D40 4-4-0 62262 leaves Auchindachy with the Keith–Craigellachie pick-up, a delightful vintage scene apart from the upper quadrant starter. ER was able to chase this in an elderly car without difficulty. 2nd August 1954. *E. Russell 363834*

Rear Cover

LYR 0F 0-4-0ST No.51218 is immaculate on a low-loader about to set sail for a railtour and then a trot round the Manchester Ship Canal system. 13th February 1967. *304212*

GNRI PPs Nos.12 and 50 team up to take a train to Londonderry from Strabane station. 22nd May 1956. *E Russell 102252*

FOREWORD

Colour-Rail is an organisation which has been known to transport enthusiasts for over thirty years. Founded and run by Ron White for most of that time, it has amassed what is probably the most comprehensive collection of colour images of rail motive power in the country. Its primary aims are to preserve as many of these images for posterity as possible and to make them available to all enthusiasts, either to purchase directly or to be able to see them in numerous books and magazines. This book would not have been possible without the countless photographers who ensured that their work was passed to an appropriate organisation to ensure its preservation. Unfortunately vast quantities of these unique historic records are consigned to the rubbish skip by those who fail to recognise their importance. If you have, or know of, collections or even single images that need a good home Colour-Rail would love to hear from you.

Paul Chancellor

October 2010

www.colour-rail.com

It's been a hard day's night for No.D8307, performing shunting duties at Malton: it's all being written down. 16th April 1968. *214903*

LMS 8P Pacific No.46225 *Duchess of Gloucester* waits at Tebay with the up 'Parly', its paintwork is fading and it's a poor job for such a lady as this. 31st August 1963. *C. J. Gammell 300451*

Images from the Colour-Rail collection have graced the pages of many books and magazines over the years but Colour-Rail has never compiled a book itself, until now. Nearly every picture on the following pages has not been seen in print before, let alone issued as a Colour-Rail slide.

Whilst the majority of images are of steam on British Railways, there are sections reflecting all the other slide series which have been issued over the years, so you will find the occasional tram, diesel and industrial interlopers along with a touch of variety from other countries as you turn the pages.

We could not include every class and location, even if we had a thousand pages, but we trust that there is something to please everyone, from the standard front three-quarter view to those fascinating images which make up so much of the collection that show the minutiae of railway operation. Then there are the road vehicles which appear in the background of so many shots along with passengers in their Sunday best, the railway workers and the 'grice' at the platform end.

The term 'grice' was one that was employed by Ron White when writing about 'spotters' in his descriptions of the various slides which have appeared in the Colour-Rail catalogue over the years, making it a 'good read' regardless of your wish to buy a slide, or not. Because those descriptions have been such a feature of Colour-Rail, it has been a pleasure to ask Ron to write most of the captions in his inimitable, humorous and sometimes caustic style.

We hope you enjoy your journey around the country and places further afield and find something new in the photographs each time you browse through the book. There is a lot to see, right down to the 'West Country' Class locomotive carrying a red-backed Western Region shed plate.

Whilst we promised you new images we would like to have one indulgence in Colour-Rail nostalgia before we start our journey, with these best sellers, as they illustrate a very important point. Here we have three of the classic classes from the Big Four, a Bulleid Pacific more or less as built, a GWR 'Castle' on a holiday express and the quite camera-shy LMS Pacific No.46220 at Euston. But rather than the expected A4 to make up the group we have a very rare colour view of the LNER Garratt No.69999. Now we would be the first to admit that this slide is not the finest in the collection but many would have thrown it in the bin. Ron White, however, recognised it for what it was, a possibly unique image of a unique locomotive, now preserved for posterity.

No.7022 *Hereford Castle* ex-works on the 18.10 Goodrington–Plymouth meets '45XX' 2-6-2T No.4561 rolling down to Newton Abbot with an up freight at the top end of Aller Junction down loop; very nice. May 1960. *P. W. Gray BRW189*

'Battle of Britain' No.34078 *222 Squadron* glowing on Ilfracombe turntable; superb. September 1961.

J. F. W. Paige BRS50.

No.46220 *Coronation* at Euston after arrival with an overnight sleeper, a fine reminder of the old Euston, beautifully lit. 1961. *BRM13*

The photographer Eric Oldham, who died recently, was a baker in Hyde and he chased this on a bicycle; the Garratt (on oil-firing trials) steamed so badly that he was able to take a whole series of pictures up to Crowden. He put the film in for processing and lost the lot due to the incompetence of the firm. The only shot which survived was this, the first shot on a new film in the camera. No.69999 heads a freight from Dewsnap up towards Dunford Bridge on the GC. 1953. *BRE140*

We start our journey in the south west of England which contained such a variety of railway operations. Not only was there the mixture of Western and Southern Regions but also the complete range of railway operations, with on the one hand a 'King' pounding up the Devon banks and on the other the single carriage train employed on the numerous tranquil branches in the area. A further contrast was the Cornish clay workings and the industrials which found employment thereon. Moving east, tank engine activity is to the fore as we head for Weymouth.

'45XX' 2-6-2T No.4565 leaves Wadebridge for Bodmin Road, her 'B' set is maroon, in the down platform is green Maunsell stock, the elegant bracket signal makes the picture. 20th April 1960. *322922*

Right
LSWR T9 4-4-0 No.30715 (wide splashers) waits at Halwill Junction with an up Padstow, Maunsell stock and a couple of swingers: what is on the down main is anyone's guess, and for Torrington? August 1960. *D. H. Beecroft, 342121.*

2MT LMS-designed 2MT 2-6-2T No.41295 backs down to her solitary coach hidden under the all-over roof of Callington station, the whole area is spotlessly clean (possibly because there were few people anywhere nearby to drop dog-ends and KFC was still half a world away). 7th August 1962. *305974*

SR Class N 2-6-0 No.31845 has the Padstow portion of the down 'Atlantic Coast Express' passing the Car-Carrier empties in their siding at Okehampton – this was a summer-only service from Surbiton (for Margo and Jerry to use, no doubt). The thought of driving a largish, new and expensive car down those narrow vans must have put one or two people off their stroke and no-claims bonus. 29th August 1964. *341498*

2MT No.41248 has a miniscule freight aiming south towards Halwill Junction, another is northwards ho! for Barnstaple Junction with no fewer than four bogies: riches indeed. 10th April 1964. *305421*

Port of Par Authority *Judy* (WB2572/1937) is dwarfed by a van which won't negotiate the tunnel that the loco was designed to do; fallacy here somewhere, I fancy. 11th September 1968. *102272*

GWR 'Manor' 4-6-0 No.7806 *Cockington Manor* leaves Dawlish with a down local, the engine is filthy; there was a water shortage in the West Country and cleaning was forbidden that summer – perhaps elbow grease was also on ration. 1959. *J. M. Mason 321463.*

GWR 'Hall' No.4948 *Northwick Hall* comes round the back of the box at Kingswear with a down stopper; the other side of the platform holds a rake of mineral empties doubtless to be filled with coal from a coaster and taken to Torquay gas works. 1958. *320982*

GWR 'Castle' 4-6-0 No.5043 *Earl of Mount Edgecumbe* (Hawksworth tender) has the 'Torbay Express' rolling into Churston station, a lovely day and who would have thought No.5043 would still be in steam in 2010. 13th September 1961. *320538*

'Warship' No.D805 *Benbow* is at an unidentified depot, there is an anonymous sign on the roof and an anonymous child surveys the machine (thinking twice about becoming an engine driver) which has been through Laira's washing plant a few times as the paint is disappearing. August 1963. *214767*

No.824 *Highflyer* does not seem to have endured too many runs through the washer since an encounter with the blue paintbrush as it comes through Dawlish with ballast, not a soul visible on promenade in high summer! 10th June 1969. *215046*

Ask a spotter to name ten places where he would expect to see a GWR '72XX' 2-8-2T and Paignton would not appear on many lists but No.7204 defies the odds and gets a day at the seaside; a lot of engine for your money. 30th August 1960. *J. R. Besley 322598*

GWR '14XX' 0-4-2T No.1466 is surprisingly grubby in plain black with the old small totem; she has just taken water and the fireman will remove the bag; a rusty fire devil guards the column. She is tucked away in the bay at the London end of the down main at Exeter St. David's and will have a gentle trot to Bampton or Dulverton as the mood comes upon her. 25th June 1963. *321782*

SR Z Class 0-8-0T No.30952 has been put on the front of an N Class to take freight from Exeter St. David's up to Central. There's probably another on the back but it's dark and we shall never know: a very atmospheric shot indeed. 1962. *A. B. Jeffery 342915*

No.5065 *Newport Castle* gets away from Exeter St. David's with down C38, a motley rake, such as can be seen of it. September 1960. *D. H. Beecroft 320590*

BR Standard 3MT 2-6-2T No.82023 drifts lazily into Sidmouth whilst a fellow classmate contemplates a journey back to the real world. Evidence of the branch freight is to the right. 26th June 1960. *381699*

No.1451 takes water at Tiverton with the 10.35 Exeter–Dulverton: the autocoach has been augmented by a brake composite. 7th September 1962. *321739*

GWR '74XX' No.7436 leaves Chard Central for the Junction, the 'B' set is augmented by a horsebox and a milk tanker, the fine all over roof covers but a single track so, if trains are to be crossed, the Taunton-bound train will force any southbound service to be backed into a siding, often the cause of alarm to strangers. August 1961. *323326*

GWR '1366' 0-6-0PT No.1370 is well down on Weymouth quay and bringing vans past a Victorian structure, lots of wrought ironwork to enjoy: we may wonder if the photographer is exceptionally tall/water resistant or merely standing on a ship. 9th October 1957. *320100*

SR 'Merchant Navy' 4-6-2 No.35006 *Peninsular & Oriental S. N. Co.* flumps into to Templecombe as only a Bulleid can. Three on with the 15.05 from Salisbury is not really exploiting the talents of this machine. 5th June 1964. *G. F. Bloxham, 343410*

Perhaps this area could best be described as the 'Strong Country'. Do you remember those adverts for beer which were passed with what seemed great frequency when travelling down from Waterloo? As well as the branch lines, once past Bournemouth going east there came the delights of Southampton and Eastleigh and of course the Isle of Wight, that oasis of antiquity and delight which was a time capsule for so many years. Beyond Portsmouth electric power ruled the roost, which we will save for another visit.

LSWR M7 0-4-4T No.30110 in the down bay at Wareham with Maunsell set 383, no lamps, no headcode, no doubt where we will go when the coal is trimmed and after the fireman has wiped his nose on the back of a grimy hand and the driver has been prised away from Page 3. 28th July 1961. *343198*

Standard 4MT 2-6-0 No.76031 delays the journeys of Mini driver, cyclist and pedestrian alike as it waits time and completion of station duties at a location which looks suspiciously like Poole. A brave soul occupies the phone box just wishing he had a device that would allow him to communicate whilst walking, oblivious to all around him, but no-one in their right mind could ever think that there would be much demand for such an item, would they? *71330*

BR 'Britannia' Pacific No.70009 *Alfred The Great* has the down 'Bournemouth Belle', 'Lord Nelson' No.30851 Sir Francis Drake waits in the bay for something to relieve, both are framed in that splendid gantry. July 1951. *S. C. Townroe 381258*

Corral Queen (ex-BR 30096, B4 Class) waddles across Belvidere Road, Southampton, new owners have fitted a cab enabling the crew to stand up without pain. Modern road transport lurks on the right. 6th April 1968. *102262*

USA 0-6-0T No.30068 crunches over Canute Road with freight for export from Southampton, not much of THAT about these days. 1960. *342245*

BR 5MT 4-6-0 No.73043 is framed in the doorway of Fratton's moth-eaten roundhouse, little used by this date except by visitors. 8th May 1966. *380072*

LSWR O2 0-4-4T No.W30 *Shorwell* rests at Wroxhall, possibly awaiting something coming through the tunnel from Ventnor. The rot has not yet set in and she still carries her nameplate and is cleanish. 12th August 1965. *341838*

M7 No.30053 (now preserved) leaves Lymington Pier with the connection for Brockenhurst. Observe the curious starting signal and vintage furniture van off to the Island. *341380*

The number of new quality images of steam in this south east corner is very limited, due mainly to the fact that colour photography really only took hold from around 1960 by which time the Kent electrification had been completed. Despite that, there were some vintage steam locomotives continuing to operate in the county alongside the latest thing in motive power, the electro-diesel. Moving up to the capital there is an encounter with the 'Brighton Belle' at Croydon whilst not far away we find something very modern.

No.E6029 (later 73 122) at Folkestone Harbour station, we don't often see this end. 15th May 1966. *208900*

0-6-0 diesel-mechanical shunter No.11220 (later to be designated as a Class 04 and numbered D2250) trudges along Dover Eastern Dock with vans, the castle high above. June 1959. *214518*

SECR H Class 0-4-4T No.31305 stands in the down main platform at Paddock Wood with the 13.00 (1 o'clock in real money) to Maidstone West, a couple of Maunsell coaches and a GUV. 10th June 1961. *340858*

N 2-6-0 No.31866 arrives in a damp Brighton with a railtour, cleaning has been attempted, but unsuccessfully. 5th December 1965. *343837*

Croydon Tram Link No.2548 on an early special working at Addington Park, the driver now modelling the obligatory high viz vest. 26th October 1999. *C. J. Gammell BUI2199*

5-BEL No.3052 threads its way out of London at East Croydon with a fellow member of the class following on behind. One had to know how to crook one's little finger when drinking tea in a first class Pullman carriage. 15th September 1963. *65391*

No.E5015 heads the 'Golden Arrow' in a very rural-looking landscape near Shortlands on a summer's day as we like to remember them, hot and sunny. 1960. *208847*

What can we say other than enjoy the Bulleid Pacifics and the supporting acts which typified the 1950s and '60s scene, plus an ominous sign of the future of steam, the diesel-hauled 'Bournemouth Belle'. Now about that red shed plate we mentioned in the introduction. Red ones were normally of the aluminium variety and carried by diesels and it is a fair bet that this one was too. When the Western Region took over the former Southern lines in the South West Plymouth Laira depot was recoded from 83D to 84A, the 83D code then being allocated to Exmouth Junction, so the chances are that all the 83D shed plates were shipped from Laira to Exmouth Junction... or are we being too logical?!

'West Country' No.34006 *Bude* and M7 30052 bask in the sun at Waterloo: the 'WC' is for Southampton with a boat train. 30th August 1961. *341370*

'WC' No.34108 *Wincanton* is ready to show that beneath all that grime there is still a powerful beast, as it sets sail for railtour duties, a last-minute substitute for a fellow class member who decided to call in sick. 19th March 1967. *G. S. Cocks, 306593*

N15 'King Arthur' 4-6-0 No.30803 *Sir Harry Le Fise Lake* (a name for young spotters to puzzle over) at Feltham, on the boil, but grubby. September 1960. *341630*

2MT 2-6-0 No.46509, in clean lined green at Clapham Junction, has a joint REC/LCGB railtour to trot round a few branches in the Thames Valley; this is Part One and the Western will insist on its two pennyworth later in the day. 25th July 1965. *304334*

'Merchant Navy' No.35020 *Bibby Line*, nice and clean amongst the apparent tank traps at Nine Elms, the old tiny totem being carried. The RCTS history of the 'Merchant Navies' tells us that No.35020 ran with this tender from 25th May to 11th July 1956 whilst engaged on dynamometer car trials between Waterloo and Exeter, it having been found that the necessary cables from the locomotive to the recording instruments could best be supported by one of the high-sided tenders. To match the lining on the cab, the sides of the tender were repainted with lowered panelling and emblem with the black top to the side sheeting. The tender was transferred to No.35028 on completion of the trials. *340059*

'Battle of Britain' No.34054 *Lord Beaverbrook* passing Woking with a down Salisbury, ten malachites in tow. 9th July 1964. *K. Fairey 343618*

'WC' No.34096 *Trevone* brings down milk empties through Woking. You never knew it was carried in four-wheel vans, did you? 28th September 1963. *M. Thompson 342815*

SR S15 4-6-0 No.30840 passing Esher with a down parcels, a little glint from a grubby locomotive as it heads towards the setting sun. 13th July 1964. *70942*

Brush Type 4 (later Class 47) No.D1926 heads the 'Bournemouth Belle' at Brookwood, Necropolis weather – all doom and gloom. July 1967 204836

Going Down from Paddington

Perhaps a Class 31 is not what everyone would expect to find as an introduction to the Western in London but they were around for a good many years in the Division. Having got over that, more traditional fare could be found at Old Oak Common and in the iconic location of Sonning Cutting with a touch of the Southern at Reading. Swinging right at Didcot there are traditional mixed traffic engines on hand at Oxford and en route to the West Midlands. The track workers at Aynho would certainly cause Health & Safety apoplexy today.

No.31 121 is insinuated into West Ealing Milk Dock – I'm sure it would prefer diesel fuel. 12th January 1976
62293

GWR '15XX' 0-6-0PT No.1503 rests in one of Old Oak's four roundhouses, so it is almost certainly Sunday, a traditional day for shed bunking. 23rd June 1963. *321817*

'Castle' No.5085 *Evesham Abbey* on an up express in Sonning Cutting, the classic shot (apart from the lack of chocolate and cream stock). 20th June 1959. *M. Thompson 320631*

SR U Class 2-6-0 No.31799 rolls into Reading South with the 12.32 from Redhill. In those days the Southern knew its place with a station at a lower level than the Western but now everything goes upstairs. 17th October 1964. *340101*

'43XX' 2-6-0 No.6302 brings an up freight under the straggly gantry at the north end of Oxford station; she hasn't seen an oily rag for a while. 4th March 1960. *322034*

No.6879 *Overton Grange* rests on Banbury shed: we never suspected there might be a 6880 one day. 12th October 1963 *321444*

2-6-0 No.7317 in plain green, and somewhat cleaner than No.6302, yields X80 in Oxford station and will totter off to the shed. Midland Compound No.1000 is on the stock but still carries the light engine code, grice congregate. 11th September 1960. *K. Fairey 323440*

No.4921 *Eaton Hall* pauses at Banbury with an up parcels, a Siphon leads the rake. 1962. *320966*

No.6970 *Whaddon Hall* plonks into Evesham with an up freight from Worcester, the ex-LMS sub-shed is seen in the background. December 1960. *321201*

GWR 'Grange' 4-6-0 No.6814 *Enborne Grange* brings freight towards Oxford passing Aynho (for Deddington). Non-health and safety has caused the PW gang to step back a couple of inches leaving a wheelbarrow in the six-foot, nobody got killed. November 1960. *321314.*

From Gloucester in the north to Frome, GWR steam is seen at work along with an industrial at Bristol hauling BR Mk1 stock, but the scene of personal memory is Swindon 'A' shop. The memories of walking through that magnificent building on a Sunday afternoon works tour copping a rare 'Castle' on the right and a 'Hall' with an 87J shedplate on the left are as vivid today as they were at the time. How could it all be swept away so that today someone can shop for a TV on the right and buy a cup of coffee on the left... and on a Sunday afternoon too!

No.3440 *City of Truro* waits in Swindon Works yard admired by a contemporary couple, he flat-hatted, tweed-jacketed, she in a floral dress and white shoes, perfect for crunching about in cinders (yes, you SHALL go the ball). 16th May 1957. *321608*

Swindon 'A' shop, boilers everywhere, not too many numbers can be read, try 2839 and 5060 for the nearer ones. 16th April 1961. *102092*

Swindon roundhouse depths reveal '2251' Class 0-6-0 No.2244 and the cab and tender of No.4930 *Hagley Hall*, another survivor, basking in the sunlight. Engine parts lay discarded on the floor, mind you don't trip over them! 21st April 1963. *J. S. Davis 322898*

'57XX' pannier tank No.9721 leaves Kemble, who knows where it will end up? Not far away, I'm sure, all the coal is on the floor, not in the bunker. March 1962. *322794*

The 'belt and braces' approach has been adopted at Gloucester shed – but which is the back-up engine for X36, No.D1056 *Western Sultan* or No.6993 *Arthog Hall*? 1963. *323313*

Port of Bristol No.S11 (P2036/1943) brings Mark 1 stock into the dock area – what is the ship, I wonder? 21st July 1963. *102260*

'57XX' 0-6-0PT No.3614 arrives at Frome with a down local, lots of passengers under the Brunel roof, but a strange headlamp placing. July 1959. *323327*.

And now for something completely different

What more can be written about the Somerset & Dorset Joint Railway? Not much, and we won't attempt to do it here. Suffice to say that the S&D had a section all of its own in the Colour-Rail catalogue.

BR 9F 2-10-0 No.92220 *Evening Star* on Green Park shed, ready for another trot to the seaside. What a waste of a good engine, permanently constrained within museum walls. 29th August 1962. *382227*

4F 0-6-0 No.44561 leaves Templecombe with an up local under juvenile supervision – this is one of the six 'Armstrongs' built specially for the S&D; the locals loved them but it didn't make them any better than the other 766 (yclept 'Big Goods' forsooth!). Sir Henry had a cunning plan to convince everyone they were better than the 3Fs (which they weren't). 16th March 1961. *300233*

'2251' Class No.3210 waits at Highbridge with the 16.00 for Templecombe, look at all those lovely totems awaiting new homes (which they probably never got). 18th August 1963. *323029*

LMS 5MT 2-6-0 No.42790 at Bath Green Park, on a Bristol local which might lead to a return to Birmingham where she belongs. An apprentice grice is shown the ropes by Grandad. 28th July 1962. *300175*

South Wales had two sheds which vied with each other to turn out clean engines for their top link work in Landore (Swansea) and Canton (Cardiff) and the handywork of the latter can be seen at Newport in the era when Canton had a small number of 'Kings' on its books. In contrast the heavy industry of South Wales produced freight traffic on a scale unimaginable today, both on the main line and through the numerous valley routes. Perhaps it was a good thing that when travelling over some of those wonderful viaducts and bridges, the passengers could not see just how little steelwork there was keeping them aloft; and the burning question of the day – where is the Walnut tree at Walnut Tree? And what is more, how did a single Southern Region-liveried carriage get into the formation of a train at Walnut Tree?

A far cry from the heavy industry of South Wales was the rural tranquillity and sparse service provided in Central Wales where 'Manors' and many BR Standard types abounded. We complete our Western tour at Shrewsbury, the meeting place not only of many lines but also an interface with the London Midland system. Indeed, before the end of steam Shrewsbury became part of that empire.

'56XX' 0-6-2T No.6643 climbs uphill over Walnut Tree Viaduct with an excursion, an SR green coach adds colour. 31st July 1965. *323322*.

'King' 4-6-0 No.6023 *King Edward II* leaves Newport with the up 'Red Dragon' – yet another Western item served with an Exhumation Order for our delectation. 27th September 1960. *E. Russell 320370*

'Britannia' Pacific No.70020 *Mercury* looks very well at Canton shed; they knew how to get a decent performance out of them (thanks to an ex LM Region shedmaster). 7th February 1960. *K. Nuttall 380116*

'42XX' 2-8-0T No.5218 clumps through Crumlin Low Level on duty K09, coal to the docks (and good quality at that), bunker first (as all downhill jobs were). It enables us to enjoy the Meccano tracery of the viaduct. 5th June 1962. *320155*

Swansea & Mumbles Car No.1 at Oystermouth: 104 seats made them really useful in the rush hours. Elsie and Doris check to see that they have the right money before boarding. 15th March 1959. *E. Russell BUI2205*

No.7800 *Torquay Manor* is percolating well and leaves Welshpool with a down local; note the siding is still laid with wartime concrete pot sleepers with tie-bars (you can't get the wood, you know). The leading coach is a Hawksworth back-breaker. *321416*

BR Class 4 4-6-0 No.75006 (double chimney) enters Dolgelly with the 14.35 from Barmouth, a charming riverside scene – the down starter is in shot but the lower arm has sadly lost the large 'S' once borne. September 1963. *380199*

No.7819 *Hinton Manor* has arrived at Machynlleth with the down 'Cambrian Coast Express', the sun shines but the clouds are threatening. 6th September 1963. *M. Thompson 321530*

No.75020, another with double chimney, gets away from Welshpool with a down local. In those days this was a real station with a fine water tower and three platforms. January 1965. *380219*

No.7821 *Ditcheat Manor* faces east at Dovey Junction having come in from Pwllheli, in the far distance is a parked DMU and a '75XXX', lots of signals and a fine feeling of the period. 21st August 1964

BR 2-6-4T No.80079 takes the pick-up eastwards from Welshpool and passes Welshpool & Llanfair Railway's *The Earl* on a Weltrol, just returned from Swindon (?) and looking very pretty. 6th October 1962. *382472*

'74XX' pannier tank No.7440 waits at Llangollen with a freight of unusual length – pity the preservation boys can't muster this size for charters (yet). August 1959. *R. Leitch 71527*

'Castle' No.5091 *Cleeve Abbey* waits at Hereford with a down parcels, the boiler has a fine oily sheen, the nameplate is scoured but the cabside plate needs attention. Behind, a fine three-post bracket signal adds to the scene, as did most Great Western items. July 1963. *323297*

BR Class 5 No.73097, resplendent in green, bangs out of Shrewsbury with a down parcels of some length, the Abbey is in the background, lots of smoke and noise. 1960. *380172*

Class 2 2-6-2T No.41209 appears to have a Severn Valley local; a spectacularly ugly Class 120 DMU has arrived, the roof is being ripped off the station and will never be the same again. 1963. *303134*

Liverpool Street for East Anglia

Taking a fictitious journey on the overnight train from Shrewsbury to London and a ride on the Circle Line finds us at Liverpool Street the next morning. This would be our first encounter with overhead electrification. Like much of Kent, East Anglia lost its steam power relatively early on in the modernisation programme and thus there are not too many colour images available to us. However, the scene at a level crossing is pure magic. The wires are up but a B1 is in charge of a train whilst a horse and cart from a previous era waits patiently to be on its way – possibly the horse is glad of the rest... With the exception of the 'Britannias' and B1s, the steam power in East Anglia had changed little in the last 50 years and it showed. We hope you enjoy your visit to the sleeper works too.

LNER B1 4-6-0 No.61362 looks a bit wan running into Liverpool Street from, possibly, Cambridge. 31st August 1961. *361745*

Right

B1s Nos.61174 and 61375 rest in Newmarket yard after bringing in race specials – more traffic lost to road. 14th October 1959. *361612*

0-6-2T N7/5 (so the combine tells us) No.69671 has the 18.00 to Enfield at Liverpool Street – note the parcels traffic still around then. 27th August 1960. 362730

GER J69/1 0-6-0T No.68599 is Stratford Works pilot, her load might well be a 'D82XX' or 'D84XX', most of which needed help most of the time. No.D5529, under a canopy of scaffolding, appears to have tried self incineration. *362389*

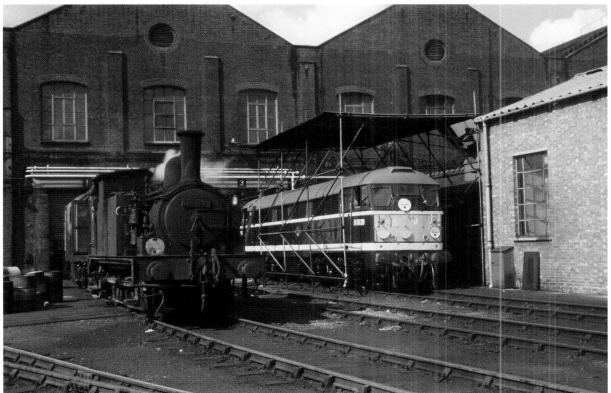

'Britannia' 7MT No.70012 *John of Gaunt* blisters through Kelvedon with an up Norwich: alas poor Tollesbury, I knew him well. 20th May 1961. *M. Thompson, 380081*

Brush Type 2 No.D5599 has come to rest in the middle of nowhere, the driver has been taken into custody by a sinister inspector. Over to you to write a comic caption... *214599*

GER J15 0-6-0 No.65389 brings the Framlingham branch freight through Marlesford station It was irreverently suggested that the local GP, Dr. Ian Allen (a railway photographer), had the line kept open to get emergency patients to Ipswich Hospital (the Mid-Suffolk Light Railway came under this category as well!) 11th February 1960. *362120*

Y3 0-4-0T No.CE41 is Lowestoft Sleeper Works shunter, though they look more like fish boxes to me. *360163*

Retracing our steps around the Circle Line we arrive at King's Cross. Will there be a 'Streak' at the buffer stops? Not today, although there is one at Top Shed but as we head up the main line towards Doncaster we seem to encounter the changing seasons as well as the usual crop of main line power.

Front ends at Top Shed: A1 No.60153 *Flamboyant* has the usual patina of York grime, A4 No.60034 *Lord Faringdon* sparkles with all the love that Dick Ball and his gang could give it. 1959. *364417*

A1 No.60123 *H. A. Ivatt* backs out of King's Cross and pauses beside the signal box; this was the first one to go, after a crash. 25th May 1964. *360354*

V2 2-6-2 No.60889 roars past Haley Wood with a down extra. It would seem that the photographer was not a hay fever victim. *363147*

9F No.92147 brings coal empties through Potters Bar; deep snow, this was a terrible winter yet trains seemed to run...? January 1963. *382006*

V2 No.60884 looks very respectable with a down special at Stevenage, the headboard (which no doubt took a while to paint) says 'West Riding Special MAYC' (or possibly MAYO), she is going across the down slow from the old Stevenage station. 26th May 1963. *M. Thompson 360155*

A1 No.60157 *Great Eastern* swarms uphill at Corby Glen with the down 'White Rose', plenty of snow around and NFI has got under the bridge for various reasons, framing the train, shading the head from the sun etc. In those days we had to work for results, not live by Photoshop. 8th January 1963. *N. F. Ingram 360549.*

A3 60083 *Sir Hugo*, in as-built condition, is ready to come off Grantham shed, express headlamps already on board. A Great Northern full brake is in the up sidings. March 1959. *D. H. Beecroft 360944*

A1 No.60158 *Aberdonian* tiptoes out of Doncaster with an up express passing 'Deltic' No.D9004 (yet to be named) newish but unfortunately slightly derailed. Help has not yet arrived, the junior grice watch and wait expectantly. *J. C. Hart 360560*

Here we celebrate 70 years of East Coast racers. Certain A4s proved quite camera-shy and No.60020 was one of them. Perhaps more surprising was that certain 'Deltics' were much less frequently photographed than others. Only with the coming of the High Speed Trains and then the Class 91s did the rarity value seem to disappear. Some collectors of Colour-Rail slides have commented that there has never been a steam slide showing the famous diamond crossing at Newcastle. Well, we don't have a steam picture in this book either, but we do at least have the diamond crossing!

A4 No.60020 *Guillemot* is amazingly clean for a Gateshead A4 (must be recently ex-works) and she will relieve A2/2 No.60502 *Earl Marischal* which has just uncoupled from an up express and looks very sordid indeed. 17th March 1957. *W. Oliver 361282*

'Deltic' No.55 007 *Pinza* comes up through Hatfield with a Hull train, blue never suited them. May 1977. *207781*

An HST leaves Newcastle and cranks hard right towards Gateshead, not a lot else to be seen save a '101' DMU and some gently rusting rails. We are up the keep, this was 6d in the old days and real value for money, unless that cutting easterly wind was blowing. 6th June 1981. *211713*

Class 91 No.91 020 slides into York, what a very dignified livery, unfortunately now destined for extinction. May 2001. *210078*

Having celebrated the racehorses we can turn the camera on the less well documented side of Eastern Region life, such as the N2 at Peterborough, just waiting for something to do, a K3 at Stamford and with more ER activity at outposts such as Nottingham and Dinting. And mind that tram.

4MT 2-6-0 No.43145 at Peterborough North, we can read 'Up the City' and 'The Lone Ranger' should we wish to, and if not how about a bit of barrow-pushing? 28th February 1959. *304725*

K3 2-6-0 No.61815 roars through Haughley with freight for Peterborough, you would not think anything agricultural could fill the skyline like this. 19th August 1959. *362582.*

B1 No.61171 has the South Yorkshire Holiday Express rumbling over the unlamented Durham Ox crossing in Lincoln – I imagine they are for Skegness and I wish them well. June 1955. *361608*

Yes, we admit it, this one has been out before but it is a pleasant view of N2 No.69571 at Peterborough, just waiting for the call to action. 10th September 1960. *J. P. Mullett BRE304*

English Electric Type 3 No.D6847, brand-new, is proudly displayed at Doncaster Works before its despatch to a hard life in the valleys of South Wales. 9th June 1963. *214690*

2-8-0s O4/8 No.63734 and O4/3 No.63712 rest on Thrumpton shed. No.63712 has a bent front frame after a night on the town, a family curse but largely ignored. *M. Thompson 362871*

BR Class 76 Bo-Bos Nos.76 028 and 76 013 bring steel into Guide Bridge; a funeral director walks beside with bowed, bared head, what did he know? 30th August 1977. *209259*

Sheffield tram No.167 is in Foregate by Cole Brothers Limited Emporium playing squash with a Morris Minor van: oh, what a grey day. 8th October 1960. *BUI2202*

GCR D11/1 4-4-0 No.62669 *Ypres* leaves Nottingham Victoria for Sheffield, passing a B1 sitting on the turntable – hard to imagine how attractive the 'Directors' once were, looking at these remains. 15th August 1960. *J. Clarke 361979*

B1 No.61169 has a couple of brake vans on the level crossing by Dinting sub-shed, viewed by a philosophical horse, cart and owner, all of some vintage. 1953. *W. Oliver 364393*.

The North Eastern Region

Strangely neglected by photographers in its day, its orange totems are now highly prized (and priced!) by today's railwayana collectors. Forgive us if we indulge a little in this under recorded area. Yes, photos of York and Leeds abound but rarely do you see views of industrial Teesside. To the unprepared traveller the journey from Middlesbrough to Redcar must have been like going to another planet as the line literally went through the middle of the steelworks where molten metal could be seen being poured just a stone's throw from the train whilst chimneys belched forth thick red 'smoke' as one freight train after another clanked along the goods lines. No highly polished racehorses here, just engines earning their keep, day after day.

V2 No.60884, seen earlier in the deep south, passes the Wakefield clock tower, background to so many pictures over the years. 1964. *363138*

Type 3 No.D6821 cranks around that fearful curve at St. Dunstan's with the 10.50 Bradford Exchange–Doncaster relief, exhaust noise about to be heard to good effect. 28th May 1967. *214662*

Fowler Class 4 tank No.42409 meanders into Wetherby with a RCTS railtour. If it stops, the peace enjoyed by the sole occupant of the platform will be severely disrupted by the flock of Lesser Tweeds as they scurry for a photographic location. 19th October 1963. *304558*

Brush Type 2/Class 31 No.5552 models 'new blue' in York yard along with a number of its less well attired friends. 30th October 1971. *214604*

York shed hosts 4MT 2-6-4T No.42548 riding the turntable, 4MT 2-6-0 No.43076 adjoins. Some walking will be required to discover the numbers of the other inhabitants. 25th August 1964. *305917*

A trio of 9Fs play dodge the sunbeam at York as the demise of steam approaches. Nos.92182, 92231 and 92249 rest together, not a Pacific in sight, hard times. 1966. *382151*.

North Eastern J26 0-6-0 No.65761 clunks through Middlesbrough with steel – willing workhorses, these. Teesside was busy then. 30th March 1962. *362241*

WD 2-8-0 No.90048 dink-donks through Eston West trying to get home before even more falls off, what stamina they had. 1st May 1962. *382070*

NER Q6 0-8-0 No.63405 bangs through Newport East with steel, industrial grot everywhere, her glands are giving generously, who cares? 13th March 1962. *362956*

Class 60 No.60 089 looks very well, cheerful indeed, approaching Saltburn from Skinningrove with steel – a modern face of the railway with the green face of Teesside. October 2003. *214554*

K1 2-6-0 No.62021 looks quite respectable at Alnwick, the fine station building reveals a Thompson coach, in the background is the Percy Memorial. 10th October 1966. *364426*

V3 2-6-2T No.67684 is Newcastle Central pilot, note the double lamp brackets over each buffer to meet Scottish requirements for weird headcode disc arrangements – note the TPO van. *364309*

J27 0-6-0 No.65879 takes empties to Camperdown Pit, a burnt smokebox was par for the course. 23rd March 1967. *S. M. Watkins 362307*

Q6 No.63459, the highest numbered one, has ventured inside Tyne Dock shed, a foolish act since little held it up save soot. The high speed move of the shed man defied the camera shutter speed. April 1966. *363000*

Having caught another night train we return to the capital for the last time and before we leave we need to visit the LT system. As well as the underground we have the Metropolitan lines and the BR steam which ran on parts of that system. Colour-Rail embraced the trams of London in its slide collection but also its Trolleybi (well, that was the plural Ron used!). However, it did not extend to London buses in those days but it does now, at least as computer downloads.

Pannier No.L91, the second one to bear that number (this had been GWR No.5757), seen here at Neasden shed with the baronial power station in the background. 26th January 1963. *102269*

Electric locomotive No.18 *Michael Faraday* in Platform 1 at Baker Street, going to the engine loop inside the tunnel to stand by. 9th May 1961. *102261*

Metropolitan A Class No.23 as restored for inclusion in Clapham Museum; it was moved to the London Transport Museum in Convent Garden. 14th January 1961. *102251*

K1-type trolleybus No.1286 turns right at an unknown place, possibly near the southern terminal of route 629, at the back of Tottenham Court Road; there's only a single set of wires. 1962. *BUI2207*

LMS Fairburn 2-6-4T No.42253 drops down on to an Aylesbury train of Metropolitan 'Dreadnought' stock, the shunter prepared to couple up straddling the live rails (as he will, about eight times an hour, each shift). Health & Safety? No, just to get on with it (as they had for too many years). 9th September 1961. *304539*

Q23 stock runs into Harrow-on-the-Hill station, this visited most of the Metropolitan system that day and here is coming in from Uxbridge. 24th August 1969. *102265*

Inside Stonebridge Park depot, a fine line-up of Bakerloo line stock; sets 3263, 3262, 3260 nearest. 3rd March 1990. *102267*

LMS Class 5 No.45217 comes past the end of Longfield Drive, Amersham, with the 12.38 Marylebone–Nottingham, the Great Central will stagger on for a while despite some dirty work to get rid of it. Now HST2 may one day be close to here, possibly in a tunnel, local Nimbys are up and running in all directions, KILL-KILL-KILL. 1st November 1961. *302779*

Should one travel from Euston or St. Pancras? Well, if you wanted to go to Birmingham then St Pancras was not much use and if Derby was your destination then perhaps you would not have fared too well going from Euston; but if you wanted to go to Manchester, well, that was a different matter. But in our case we are just visiting the termini and sheds so we had better go to Euston and St. Pancras.

LMS Fowler 3P 2-6-2T No.40026 stealthily approaches stock in St. Pancras station, she is station pilot and will remove the coaches to the sidings, a job just within the powers of this 'Surface Raider' or 'Bread Van', as they were known. The running-in board features and the five gasholders which had Preservation Orders on them failed to survive (as might be expected). *302081*

LMS 'Patriot' 4-6-0 No.45548 *Lytham St. Annes* on up W521 is about to dive into Northchurch Tunnel, she still has steam on after a couple of miles over Tring Summit, going well, but will she ever be cleaned again? 10th January 1960. *301776*

LMS 'Princess Royal' Pacific No.46207 *Princess Arthur of Connaught* is ready to back down to Euston for an evening express to the north, immaculate apart from overuse of the pep-pipe (shame). 23rd August 1961. *J. G. Dewing 300809.*

'Black Five' No.44846 and 'Jubilee' No.45597 *Barbados* rest in Kentish Town roundhouse, enough sunlight to reveal all. 14th June 1962. *A. G. Forsyth 304285*

For an area of such intense railway activity the Midland lines around Birmingham seem to have received scant attention and Wolverhampton even less. We have yet to find a colour photograph taken in the steam era at Wolverhampton High Level, for instance, so we will not be going there on this trip! Much of the East Midlands seems to have fared little better. In fact, those taking colour photographs in the 1950s and '60s much preferred pointing their cameras at big green (or red) engines than at the humble 8F or Class 5 (or their counterparts in South Wales and the North East) – but give them an 0F or 1F and they were as happy as Larry (who was Larry?).

Midland 2P No.40585 is all coaled up and ready to go at Nottingham shed – but perhaps not today and the rusty wheels suggest it might not have gone out yesterday, either. January 1960. *302133*

Rebuilt LMS 'Royal Scot' 4-6-0 No.46140 *The King's Royal Rifle Corps* on Leicester GC shed, polished, whitened buffers, lent by Kentish Town for what, I assume, was a special working (Cup Final?). The picture is undated, like so many that we have saved. *J. M. Mason 304489*

Midland 2F 0-6-0 No.58271 has been summoned from deep sleep to pilot W721 round some of Birmingham's forgotten and forgettable corners, she has been nicely cleaned and is being admired by all. *304118*

7P 'Royal Scots' Nos.46160 *Queen Victoria's Rifleman* and 46132 *The King's Regiment (Liverpool)* have been reallocated to Saltley where they are being admired by grice, they are amazingly clean for the period and it is to be hoped their nameplates will be refitted and improve things further. Saltley never had anything so good before. *301030*

Former London, Tilbury & Southend Railway 3P 4-4-2T No.41975 is ready for anything at Seaton Junction (even if that is but a gentle stroll to Uppingham with a single coach). *J. M. Mason 302117*

MR IF 0-6-0T No.41734 carries the full cab and is well polished at Staveley Works; the hiring agreement still has a few years to run. Note the bent dart carried on the front footplate, not in the usual place. 1961. *J. M. Mason 304185*

BR 9F No.92028, an ex-Crosti (no, we are not going to do the Parrot sketch here), rests in the shed yard at Kettering, so neatly placed behind the up platform, reducing the chance of ignominious rejection by the foreman to a minimum. Incredible that with such massive ironmongery to hand the 4F appreciation society should have bred and flourished here (and remains in full voice today despite all attempts to show them the light). January 1965. *381034*

0F 0-4-0ST No.47007 stands in one of the quarries served by the Cromford & High Peak, a rather suave guard lays down the law, a shunter (with massive toothpick) absorbs knowledge. The driver awaits Jove's thunderbolt, now read on... *300205*

Destinations from Crewe

A different view of Conway is all that we are to see of North Wales this time before arriving at Crewe via Macclesfield. No doubt those of a Midland persuasion would have the same feelings about a Sunday afternoon at the works here as would our friend at Swindon earlier, but at Swindon they did not keep a steam tram at the works.

Three different types of West Coast main line power are on hand in the form of the first main line diesel, possibly the last express diesel locomotives to be built for use in this country and the electrics which replaced them. A plethora of steam was to be found in the Manchester area and this was well recorded by the cameramen of the day as we are now approaching the area where steam made its last stand.

There is a 'Pug' that is trying to escape by crossing the road whilst the Liverpool Overhead Railway continues to provide a public facility. Back on the main line to the north west we approach Preston.

BR 4MT 4-6-0 No.75012 blows off emerging from Conway Bridge with a down express (so the slide mount says). Nice blue sea, wish you were here! 1959. *380852*

4F 0-6-0 No.44310 takes a life-giving drink at Congleton Lower Junction, three of sand and two brake vans have proved a sore trial to her; might she now have to go to Biddulph Street Goods, on the far side of the embankment and viaduct? I'm lost! August 1963. *303869*

LMS Stanier 2-6-4T No.42458 enters Macclesfield Central with a local from Stockport, she has a Standard 4 chimney (as if you cared). November 1957. *301981*

'Jubilee' No.45572 *Eire* has received works attention at Crewe and is being tidied up before being reunited with her tender. Class 5 No.45488 behind her has far to go, still a symphony of rusty platework yet with shiny lined black paint as well – odd. 30th May 1954. *E. Russell 301163*

A busy scene at Manchester Central of blessed memory, four in a line: far left Stanier 4P No.42479 lurks behind the fine running-in board, another, No.42560, is the main subject with a down express (yes!), Fowler 2-6-2T No.40018 cringes next to her and in the shadows of the canopy 'Britannia' No.70017 *Arrow* has the up 'Palatine' – we also see the fine overall roof now turned to secular purposes. 1962. *302005*

The Ince Tram locomotive waits her fate in Crewe Works yard, I don't know what happened to her, one of life's little mysteries. 18th February 1962. *304253*

'Jubilee' No.45642 *Boscawen* and 5MT No.45306 have the 07.00 to Barrow and 08.00 to Blackpool at Preston, ratty specimens both but the early bird has caught the worm. 30th May 1964. *P. A. Fry 301363*

5MT No.45234 has the 17.22 to Blackpool at Manchester Victoria, a magnificent night shot, really well exposed, plenty of detail in the motion, yet the station lights have not gone too far, the colour light signals warm the steam. It would be nice if we could credit the photographer, but we can't, only respectfully raise our hats to Anon. December 1966. *305864*

Diesel-electrics Nos.10001/10000 have the down 'Royal Scot' at Crewe, it's a typical summer's day, hissing down. 20th June 1957. *214989*

No.E3043 (84 003) in electric blue with cast crest, another handsome livery that was too good to keep – here seen at Southport so perhaps it won't be racing today. *214831*

Class 50 No.404 at Crewe, hopefully in working order, but then they did usually hunt in pairs. 19th April 1970. *214522*

Speedy they might be but so claustrophobic – bring back the Mk1 behind a (tilting) 'Duchess'. Class 390 at near Leighton Buzzard, 30th January 2010. *P. Chancellor 299938*

LYR 2P 2-4-2T No.50850, rebuilt with Belpaire boiler, comes off Newton Heath shed; last survivor of her class, she makes a lovely picture, but don't think that is a conventional dome securing device. 1961. *302173*

4P Compound No.41190 has an impressive layer of mud over her once lined black livery as she climbs away from Chapel-en-le Frith with a local for Buxton, the leading coach in blood and custard is of some age and interest. 2nd April 1957. *W. Oliver 301807*

3F 0-6-0T No.47480 at Newton Heath, 'Jinty', 'Jocko' or 'Dobbin', depending on whence you came, the shunter seeks a lift. 3rd December 1964. *304033*

8F 2-8-0 No.48490 on freight at Furness Vale, crossing another, fine signals all round and a viaduct afar off. 3rd December 1957. *W Oliver 303428*

4F Nos.44490 and sister 44076 at Springs Branch shed, the former is dirty, the latter cleaned to the degree that a faint LMS has appeared on the tender, hardy survivor. 23rd March 1963. *303911*

3F No.47550 shuffles around Bank Hall yard (always a difficult shed to bunk). This high level view shows the top of the locomotive and how the coal can get into unexpected places. *304045*

LYR 0F 0-4-0ST No.51204 emerges from a warehouse at Irwell Street, Salford, guarded by a flagman – this was (in 1960) part of railway life, ten years later, forgotten. *304198*

Liverpool Overhead Railway set No.41 sweeps in to Wapping, a solitary punter waits. 1954. *102174*

2F No.51371, Aspinall saddle tank rebuild of a Barton Wright 0-6-0, blows off furiously waiting to leave Newton Heath shed for sidings unknown in the hinterland of Miles Platting. 1960. *304131*

4P No.42665 shunts in the dead of night at Preston, the locomotive needs a clean to give optimum reflection but, at this time in the life of steam, may not get one. 28th December 1966. *300109*

'Crab' No.42794 near Charnock with a returning Blackpool job, the fireman has a sit down after polluting half of Lancashire. 1962. *303690*

'Britannia' No.70012, looking rather less cared for than when seen at Kelvedon earlier, blasts past Lancaster No.1 box with an up Barrow train, sound and fury, and one in the front coach wants it all and will probably get it (in his hair, eyes, navel...). 1966. *A. E. R. Cope 380509*

Wide Open Spaces

There is a lot of country between Preston and the Scottish border and the tales of camping out overnight to get classic shots on Shap and the Settle & Carlisle line are legendary. The sound of a train headed by a 'Duchess' and banked from Tebay in the light of a still dawn will remain with those who were there for ever. Unfortunately the 'Duchesses' did not make it to the end, replaced by grimy but gloriously vocal 'Britannias', but just listen to that chime whistle on the wind... Just sit back and enjoy the journey to Carlisle via whichever route you fancy.

5MT No.45056 and 'Jubilee' No.45742 *Connaught* stop at Penrith with up 1M38, the 14.00 Glasgow–Liverpool. See BRM 2456 for the departing shot: Chris must have moved well to get to the later position and regain his breath. July 1964. C. J. Gammell, *302624*

5MT No.45259 thumps past Kirkby Stephen West with the 05.52 Carlisle–Stourton, a nice exhaust and the fireman beams with satisfaction at the photographer. 19th May 1964. *302820*

'Britannia' No.70024 on the down Horse & Carriage at Grayrigg, a tremendous load, 22 bogies and various six- and four-wheelers, banked by ex-works No.42210, all of which can be seen on a TVP video, taken by my old schoolmate Jim Bowler, working well in the foreground. The noise was wonderful and audible for many minutes before the cavalcade appeared; the pain of an overnight pre-M6 drive in an Austin A40 receded rapidly and it turned into a great weekend. 30th August 1966. *380713*

4MT 2-6-0 No.43028 bangs out of Oxenholme and has got as far as Peat Lane with iron ore empties which she will take to Tebay and then on to the Stainmore line for a refill somewhere on Teesside. *303035*

Fowler 2-6-4T No.42396 banks at Scout Green, passengers risk strangulation trying to get through the vent simultaneously. 13th August 1960. *E. Russell 301953*

'Britannia' No.70049, formerly *Solway Firth*, has been attacked by oily rags and looks very well despite the loss of her plates. *P. Riley 380611*.

B1 No.61278 at Carlisle has been cleaned to a certain extent and is now required to take a special over the Waverley Route; she wasn't terribly struck on the idea but got there eventually. 3rd December 1966. *363687*

No.42313 is station pilot at Citadel. Once she carried the name *The Prince* after a royal visit to Derby, prestige! 1960. *J. C. W. Halliday 30189*

More wide open spaces greet the traveller going north from Carlisle but our route takes us around the coast via Dumfries, Stranraer and Ayr. Moving east through Waverley territory we come to Edinburgh where, at least in the early 1960s, the contrast between Haymarket and St. Margarets sheds could not have been more marked. At Haymarket there was space and clean green motive power in abundance. At the other end of the city were small grubby engines squeezed into a site through which the main line passed with drivers, cleaners and spotters using a foot crossing between the two parts at their peril, but unless you know otherwise, all survived without the need for paling fencing, flashing lights and sirens!

'Crab' No.42737 leads an anonymous 'Black 5' out of Ayr for Newcastle. This has come from Butlin's at Heads of Ayr camp and may well get home via the Port Road, Carlisle and Hexham, a nice thought. September 1962. *J. B. Snell 305622*

'Crab' No.42918 is remarkably clean but is parked outside the lifting bay at Stranraer shed, she may have run warm coming over from Ayr. 17 September 1959. *J. S. Davis 304995*

5MT No.45472 passing Beattock Summit box with an up freight, ten miles of coasting and hope she hasn't got the axle-box thump which bedevilled so many of these and bruised so many rib cages. 1959. *305560*

LNER A2 Pacific No.60535 *Hornets Beauty* stops at Dumfries with a Carlisle train, unloved, hived off by Haymarket to Polmadie (who didn't wish to know and left her and others out the back of the shed to fester away). 1964. *363302*

No.70018 *Flying Dutchman*, complete with Western Region route disc, waits at Galashiels with a northbound passenger. Parcels have been loaded and helpful juvenilia shift the barrow; observe the lovely gardens so typical of the pride staff once had. It won't be decade before all this has gone and a ring road (unlovely) will be a replacement. Now 50 years after this was taken there are still dreams of reopening some of the Waverley Route. 30th September 1961. *102175*

WD 2-10-0 No.90755 makes an interesting partner for NBR J36 No.65306 on Grangemouth shed, each equally useful, yet the little one gave four times as much service as the WD! 12th June 1962. *382435*

A3 No.60101 *Cicero* moves off Haymarket shed to take the 'Heart of Midlothian' southwards (but not beyond Newcastle). This was the A3 everyone wanted (after the four from Carlisle Canal). May 1959. *D. H. Beecroft 363305*

NBR J88 0-6-0T No.68338 looks very well at St. Margarets, despite having more coal on the cab roof than in the bunker; the 64A debating society is in full voice surrounded by green machines. *J. S. Davis 364110*

Trams abounded in Scotland and here we view of few of them. As the last tracks were pulled up it would have been a brave soul who would have predicted (after a wee dram) trams in Edinburgh in the 21st century.

A gaggle of Glasgow trams roosting in their nest, the Dalmarnock depot roofless after a fire in 1961 and the last Glasgow tram depot in 1962. *BUI2204*

Glasgow tram No.82 in George Square preceded by a Standard Vanguard(?) rust-bucket which would have a job to keep in front if the tram was wound up. Nice hat too! *BUI2206*

Aberdeen tram No.33, and a nice Standard 8 or 10, in Union Street, the Granite City indeed. 1956. *BUI2207*

Edinburgh tram No.253 and another outside Binns: look at those cars, an Armstrong-Siddeley and a Humber. 31st July 1954. *E. Russell BUI2209*

In the hustle and bustle of Glasgow there were no fewer than four major terminal stations not to mention sheds galore and two locomotive works. A full day could easily be spent 'doing the rounds' and recording at least 500 locomotives on a Sunday. Photographers again expressed their preferences with untold pictures taken at Polmadie – but Corkerhill, no. Almost all of the rarest 'Jubilees' on film were based at Corkerhill including Ron's holy grail No.45711 – he is still hunting for that elusive shot! But Glasgow was not just about big engines, witness the industrial running down the main road with traffic all around.

No.46249 *City of Sheffield* brews up for the climb to 'The Shilford', the start from St. Enoch which the old Glasgow & South Western Railway regarded as a problem to be solved, but which a 'Duchess' on the evening 'Parly' to Carlisle wouldn't notice. July 1963. *J. B. Snell 305047*

'Jubilee' No.45588 Kashmir on Corkerhill shed, someone has cleaned just enough of the cabside to allow the dreaded yellow stripe to be applied. 10th August 1964. *305103*

NBR J37 0-6-0 No.64563 with a V3 tank at Parkhead shed, which saw rather less attention from photographers than the main ones. May 1959. *D. H. Beecroft 363332*

Fairfield Shipbuilding's little electric saunters down the Govan Road drawing power from the trolleybus wires, not a lot of that sort of thing in the UK. 27th April 1960. *102263*

A4 No.60024 *Kingfisher* backs off Buchanan Street for St. Rollox shed, she'll be serviced, turned and back to Aberdeen quite quickly. Catch a coach to the Granite City from the same spot today, see how long that takes. May 1966. *363608*

No.46201 *Princess Elizabeth* makes a clean start from St. Enoch on the 17.30 to St. Pancras. May 1962. *305972*

No.45729 *Furious* has another stopper leaving St Enoch, destination unknown. 21st April 1962. *D. J. Dippie 305152*

A view inside Cowlairs Works where BR 6MT 4-6-2 No.72006 *Clan Mackenzie* is the only identifiable ironmongery. Shortly she will be a gleaming machine once more, who waived the magic wand? 21st May 1961. *382504*

No book would be complete without a visit to Fort William and the West Highland area and we are not about to disappoint but the stunning photographs taken on today's charters were few and far between in the 1950s and '60s. On the east side of Scotland Dundee and Perth provided a rich mixture of LMS and LNER power. Indeed Perth was one of the few places where one could regularly see 'Duchesses' and A4s together when the A4s operated the Glasgow–Aberdeen three-hour expresses. And if you liked Stanier Class 5s then again Perth was the place to be, having the largest allocation of any shed in the country at one time.

Completing our mainland journey we find ourselves in the far north where dieselisation came early. At least the North British Type 2s gave Ron plenty of scope for comment when it came to writing his captions.

Standard 4MT No.80126 is halfway up the bank from Killin to Killin Junction, the load is not taxing. 14th August 1962. *382375*

K1/1 No.61997 *MacCailin Mor* sends up a great plume of smoke, 5MT No.44973 (a non-smoker) gets down to the turntable and fresh air. 7th September 1959. *363341*

LNER K2 2-6-0s Nos.61764 *Loch Arkaig* and 61791 *Loch Laggan* have been put to bed on the loch side at Fort William shed: their chimneys differ. 10th September 1959. *M. Thompson 364147*

Caledonian 2F 0-6-0 No.57264 is south of Perth, alongside the shed, clean with a capped chimney, amongst fine signals – how pleasant. May 1959. *D. H. Beecroft 305004*

J38 0-6-0 No.65931 regains the main line at Throsk, coming in round the back of the box, the 'Caledonian Forth Bridge' just fails to creep into the picture. *364035*

No.46226 *Duchess of Norfolk* leaves Perth with a very short fish/parcels, a 2P could manage this (for a while). 13th April 1963. *305017*

'Jubilee' No.45737 *Atlas* has 2F No.57580 for company on Perth Shed, grice hover for good luck by the ladder. *305155*

A3 No.60096 *Papyrus* is standing pilot at Dundee shed, clean enough, the time of the A2s is not yet come. 1960. *363514*

A4 No.60009 *Union of South Africa* passing Blackford with a down Aberdeen; the storm passed just in time. 1965. *363563*

5MT Nos.45192 and 45496 have the 08.30 Inverness–Edinburgh on the climb to Culloden Viaduct, going well. 28th August 1959. *304988*

NBR J37s Nos.64577 and 64624 rest knee-deep in the ashes at Dundee Tay Bridge shed: fine strong machines, these. November 1965. *363969*

No.D6156, a North British Loco.Co. Type 2, is reversing a tiny freight from the main, apparently on to a branch – all lines are fully signalled with upper quadrants. There's an unreadable cast iron notice (with a leaning bicycle) and I have a vague feeling this is on the old Great North of Scotland Railway – yet another of the thousands of pictures we hold where the photographer was going to get round to identification (but never did). *214586*

Highland Railway 'Jones Goods' No.103 sallies forth from Thurso on railtour duty whilst D5115 will set off later to look for the other half of its mini snow plough. *201073*

A1 No.60161 *North British* rolls into Stonehaven with the 19.45 Aberdeen–York, you'd have thought they would have kept this one clean at Haymarket. 9th August 1963. *P. A. Fry 363368*

J36 No.65265 outside Inverurie Works: in the last years of steam they did some lovely work on older engines and this was a prime specimen. 1964. *363896*

Irish railway scenes have long been a feature of the Colour-Rail collection, providing endless fascinating scenes. Definitely a country of contrasts – we had LMS look-alike tank engines and relatively modern traction operating in the North whilst as a total contrast narrow gauge lines employing ancient steam motive power and 'buses on rails' plied their trade elsewhere to a timetable which bore little resemblance to reality. You may not know, however, that Colour-Rail once used to sell slides featuring 'foreign' railways, so we have included a small selection from 'the rest of the world' which almost complete our Colour-Rail journey.

GNRI S2 Class 4-4-0 No.190 *Lugnaquilla* is ready to leave Strabane for Belfast, this is more like it. 19th May 1959. *C. J. Gammell 102257*

Ex-SL&NCR No.27 *Lough Erne* shunts Belfast Docks. August 1965. *102255*

GNRI SGS3 No.48 is serviced at Amiens Street shed, Belfast. August 1961. *D. H. Beecroft 102258*

A railcar set sweeps into Lisburn, this is the 17.15 from Belfast Great Victoria Street, not conventionally pretty. 2nd June 1975. *102264*

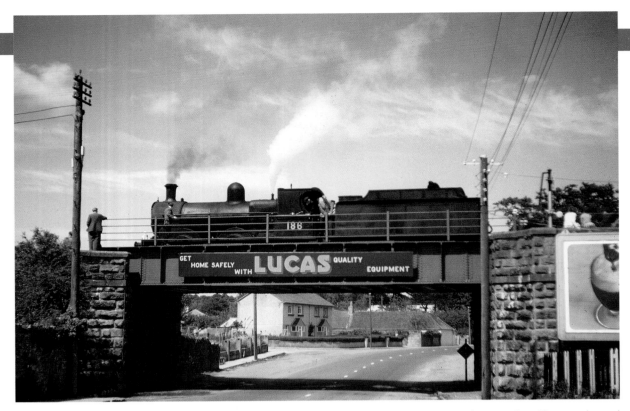

CIE J15 Class No.186 stands on the bridge at Cahir, she was only a girl of 85 when this was taken, another 45 years plus and she is still around. 7th June 1964. *102259*

CIE B4 Class 464 has been tagged on to diesel C231, who helps whom? 4-6-0 tanks are very rare animals indeed. 1960. *102256*

County Donegal No.2 *Blanche* and No.3 *Meenglass* at Ballyshannon, last excursions await. 3rd August 1959. *E. Russell 102268*

CIE G2 Class 654 at Ballaghaderreen with the branch train, stone age beasts and lovely with it. 1961 *102266*

The Hill of Howth repair car No.11 at Sutton – incroyable, as they say in the Common Market. 1953. *102254*

County Donegal railcar No.10 has trailer No.5 and a van in tow entering remote Lough Esk station going home to Stranrolar. 19th May 1956. *E. Russell 102273*

4-4-0 No 60 trundles its ancient stock out of Portadown on a beautiful August day in 1964 but the star of the show are those two signal gantries. *A A Jarvis 102270*

Belfast Tram No.423 in Great Victoria Street station. The advert on the side was obviously drawn up by a visionary advertising man for Kraft. September 1953. *BUI2208*

No.B5204 (Hartmann *3316/1908*) is ready for whatever might turn up at Purwokerto, logged up and ready to be transferred to someone's pre-war Hornby tinplate layout (or even Bing), since both seemed to have a rich variety of 0-4-0 tender locomotives pretending to be something else. 1970.

No.5918 *Mount Gelai* is stopped near Meninzau for some very late visitors to record East African Railway's finest Garratt on a final run of A38 down to Mombasa. This locomotive seemed to be the personal fiefdom of the Singh brothers who kept her in such prime condition that she was the obvious candidate for preservation. 19th February 1977. *D. H. Beecroft*

We may complain about short trains and over-crowding, and will Cross-Rail ever get finished, but in Nepal they cope, no matter what, inside, outside, above, below, rain, sun, snow; but it was all too much for the engine which eventually expired and had to be rescued by a passing Bagnall. Janakpurdham, 27th November 1984. *Hugh Ballantyne*

Mouses/Mice/Meece? Nos.001 (Hartman *1132/1881*) and 004 (Cockerill *1602/1890*) at Entroncamento shed where they both undertook pilot duties. These enchanting little beasts would fit on to the turntable with whatever other locomotive they might be required to draw out from the roundhouse. They were well tanks of very limited capacity and the filler arrangements were slightly different, taller on 001- both could be filled using a standard bathroom jug if the water column could not be reached. 9th May 1964.

25NC No.3423 *Victoria* is getting a bit run-down but still capable of shifting freight across the Karoo; a little patience would have an afternoon thunderstorm turn up to make a really seductive backdrop at Witput. Keep working away until sundown, then retire to the Grange Hotel for a few soothing beers and a good dinner followed by night tape recording, but bear in mind the generator goes off at midnight and it is pitch dark out there (especially if you've fallen asleep in the bath!). August 1976.

Sunset (and afterglow) on South African steam as GMAM No.4111 on a northbound freight waits at paradise (Paradys) to meet another on the last lap in from Mafeking to Vryburg. She stood there for some time and the exposure had come down to 1/8th of a second at f1.8 (handheld – how clean living we were in those days). May 1988.

Just one series of slides remain to be represented, this being 'Preservation'. Over 300 slides were issued in this series but sales were always slow. Nonetheless it is just as important to save such images for the future as it is to keep those from previous eras, for in due course they too will form an important historic archive source.

GWR 'Dukedog' 4-4-0 No.9017 makes a very convincing recreation of the 1950s as it meanders between Llangollen and Carrog. One of the first main line locomotives to be rescued from extinction, it has taken longer to return it to its homeland in an appropriate livery than it ran in service for its main line owners. *P. Chancellor*

'Gods Wonderful Railway' or 'Great Way Round'? Ron White expressed some very outspoken views on all things Copper Capped but despite his efforts the spirit of the Great Western refuses to die, although perhaps No.7802 *Bradley Manor* is a little bit 'over the top' in its representation of the past.
P. Chancellor

2010 saw the 50th anniversary of standard gauge preservation. Winding the clock back to 1960 when the Middleton and Bluebell Railways started their operations, we find two enthusiasts in conversation, one making predictions for the year 2010 and he said:

- The Bluebell Railway will be home to two Bulleid Pacifics and a 9F.
- 8P power representing the Big Four and the BR Standards will operate trains over the national network week in and week out.
- Hundreds of former BR locomotives will be restored and operated on preserved lines across the country.
- Heritage lines will be recognised as essential to the local economy in many areas of the country.
- A completely new main line express passenger locomotive will be built and operate across the network drawing huge crowds.

And his friend said "Do you also see a flying pig passing by?"

'Flying Pig' No.43106 celebrates 40 years of public services at the Severn Valley Railway, May 2010. *P. Chancellor*